Visit http://powerof10math.com/
to find correlating teaching
resources as well as other free
downloads you can use
with this book.

For other book inquiries
please contact:
Deanna Zevin at
dzevin@saugususd.org

This book is dedicated to our children and to all of our students past, present, and future.

This book belongs to

_____

Once upon a time (not that long ago), a boy named Doogie McDoogle daydreamed throughout most of his elementary math instruction, never thinking it would be needed in his life.

Like many of his friends, Doogie dreamed of becoming a professional basketball player in the NBA. In fact, it was all he ever thought about.

"I'm NEVER going to use this," mumbled Doogie in the First Grade when his homework was returned with minus marks and frowny faces.

"I'm NEVER going to use this!" grumbled Doogie in the Third Grade.

"I'm NEVER going to use this!" groaned Doogie in the Sixth Grade. "What good is math when I need to be thinking about my lay-ups?" Basketball was all Doogie thought about, and his math scores showed it.

As his passion for basketball grew more intense, Doogie realized that if he wanted to be a real professional basketball player he would need a real leather basketball. One day, while looking through his favorite sports magazine, Doogie read an advertisement for genuine leather basketballs at Nick's Sporting Goods.

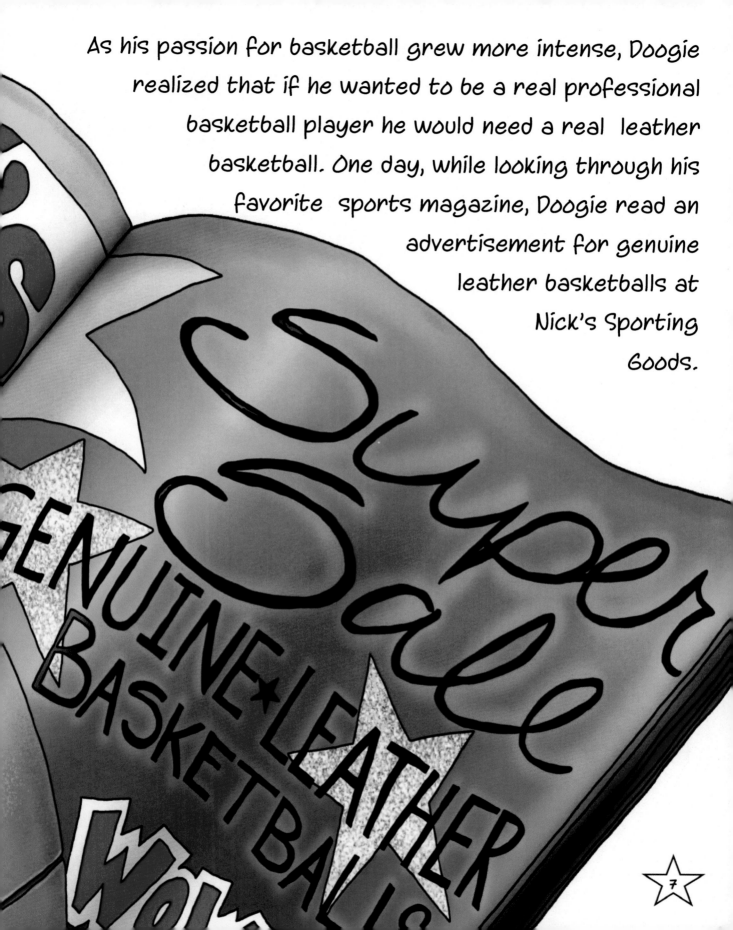

When he was sure he had enough money, Doogie went to buy his new basketball. Upon entering the store Doogie noticed a group of classmates known at school as the 'Brain Gang'. These kids always knew the correct answers to the hardest math problems and they liked to make fun of Doogie when he didn't get the classwork right. Doogie nervously hoped they hadn't noticed him come into the store.

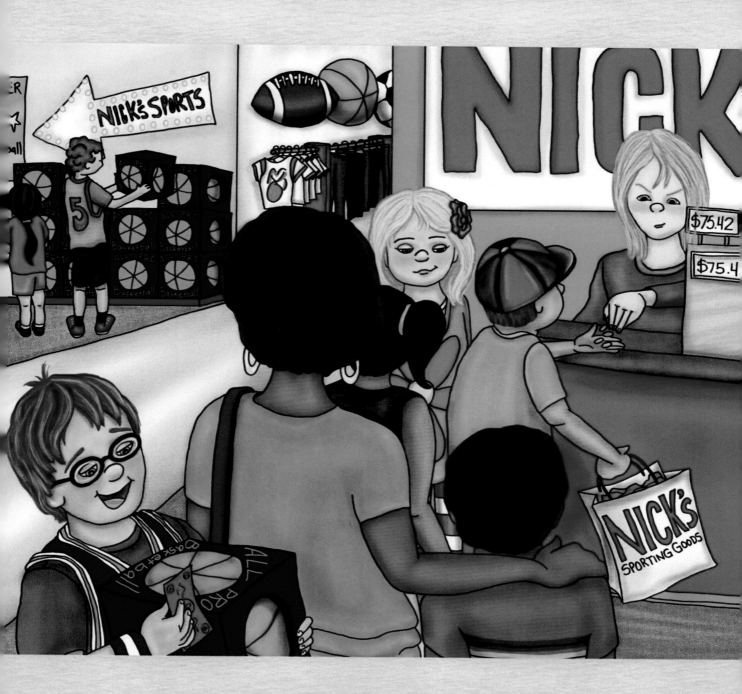

As he set the ball on the check-out counter and handed the clerk his money, Doogie was shocked when she burst out in laughter.

"Are you kidding me?" she asked sarcastically.

A flush of red hot embarrassment raced through Doogie's body, but he didn't know what she meant.

"Try again when you've got the right amount of money!" she cackled.

Doogie quickly turned to race out of the store,
barely missing the 'Brain Gang' as he ran
through the doors.

To make matters worse, in his quick escape,
Doogie tripped and fell flat on his face.

He felt humiliated as people all around him began
to laugh.

Suddenly, in a cloud of smoke and with a loud bang, Doogie is taken aback by the sudden appearance of a pint-sized superhero.

"Who are you?" Doogie yelps.
I am Tenacious Ten and I come
from the planet Numeropolis
where all the children
love math and the
power of numbers."

"What kind of name is 'Tenacious'?" asks Doogie.
Ten replies, "Tenacious means 'I never give up and nor
should you'. I have super powers that allow me to help
the children of this Universe who are suffering from
math anxiety – those children who are seriously confused
but are too embarrassed to ask for help. The words
'I just don't get it!' are my Call to Arms!"

"I saw what happened, Doogie, and I can help you understand your problem," exclaims Ten.

Feeling a little unsure, but too upset to question why this strange girl is talking to him, he replies, "I just don't get it. The sign read $5, but when I tried to pay the clerk she just laughed at me."

"What we have here, Doogie, is a place value problem.
The same digits don't always have the same value.
Let me show you."

Ten pulls out a place value chart from her super power pouch. At that moment, a black circle jumps out of her pocket and says, "This is clearly a job for me! Just call me Deci."

Ten exclaims to Doogie,

"You don't know how powerful this little decimal is."

Feeling proud, Deci replies, "I can turn $5 into

$500 with only two little moves!"

Ten continues ..., "In our place value system, we use the same digits over and over again. There are only ten: 0, 1, 2, 3, 4, 5, 6, 7, 8, and 9. It's where you PUT them that matters. The price of the basketball was 50 dollars, or 5 – 0, <u>not</u> 5."

10×10×10	10×10	10		$\frac{1}{10}$
THOUSANDS	HUNDREDS	TENS	ONES	DECIMAL	TENTH
10^3	10^2	10^1	10^0		10^{-1}

Doogie scratches his head as he says, "Hmmm, but doesn't zero have NO value? It's zilch, zip, nothing, nada, right?"

Just then 'Zero', a loud-mouthed donut shaped character somersaults out of Ten's power pocket.

$\frac{1}{10 \times 10}$ HUNDREDTHS 10^{-2}	$\frac{1}{10 \times 10 \times 10}$ THOUSANDTHS 10^{-3}	$\frac{1}{10 \times 10 \times 10 \times 10}$ TEN THOUSANDTHS 10^{-4}	$\frac{1}{10 \times 10 \times 10 \times 10 \times 10}$ HUNDRED THOUSANDTHS 10^{-5}	

"Whoa buddy, no value?" shouts Zero. "You've got me all wrong! I do a mighty big job. I am known in the math business as a <u>placeholder.</u> You can't just ignore me! I hold the spot that allows the other digits to get into their right place. When you read the price of the basketball, didn't you see ME? I'm the one who pushed the '5' up to the 'tens' place, making it a $50 basketball!"

Deci argues, "Hold on a minute. Without me, Zero, you couldn't do your job! I am the most important symbol!"

	ONES	DECIMAL	$\frac{1}{10}$ TENTHS		$\frac{1}{10 \times 10}$ HL
10^0			10^{-1}		10^{-2}

10			$\frac{1}{10}$		$\frac{1}{10 \times 10}$		$\frac{1}{10 \times 10 \times 1}$
TENS	ONES	DECIMAL	TENTHS		HUNDREDTHS		TH
10^1	10^0		10^{-1}		10^{-2}		10^{-3}

Zero responds, "Without a placeholder,

you are nothing, just a dot!"

In unison, Deci and Zero shout,

"Doogie, who do you think is more important?"

Doogie sighs, "I still don't get it!"

10 TENS 10^1	ONES 10^0	DECIMAL	$\frac{1}{10}$ TENTHS 10^{-1}	$\frac{1}{10 \times 10}$ HUNDREDTHS 10^{-2}	$\frac{1}{10 \times 10}$ T 10^{-3}

Zero puffs up importantly, "Watch what I can do! They don't call me 'ZERO THE HERO' for nothing!"

	100	10			$\frac{1}{10}$	$\frac{1}{10 \times 10}$	$\frac{1}{10 \times 10}$
NDS	HUNDREDS	TENS	ONES	DECIMAL	TENTHS	HUNDREDTHS	THOU
	10^2	10^1	10^0		10^{-1}	10^{-2}	10^{-3}

"Without me all you had was $5," continues Zero.
"But look what happens when I step in to the
'ones' place and push the 5 over to the 'tens'
place – you now have $50!"

	100	10			$\frac{1}{10}$	$\frac{1}{10 \times 10}$	$\frac{1}{10 \times 10}$
ANDS	HUNDREDS	TENS	ONES	DECIMAL	TENTHS	HUNDREDTHS	THO
	10^2	10^1	10^0		10^{-1}	10^{-2}	10^{-3}

Ten adds, "Doogie, if you push the 5 to the 'hundreds' place, its value would be 500.

ANDS	100 HUNDREDS 10^2	10 TENS 10^1	ONES 10^0	DECIMAL	$\frac{1}{10}$ TENTHS 10^{-1}	$\frac{1}{10 \times 10}$ HUNDREDTHS 10^{-2}	$\frac{1}{10 \times 10 \times 10}$ THOUSAND 10^{-3}

We would write that number with two zeroes to the right of the 5. One zero holds the 'ones' place and the other holds the 'tens' place, making it 500.

Even though your bill has a 5 on it the value of your bill is 5 – ONES. Your basketball cost $50. You would need 50 – ONES to buy it."

Doogie, beginning to see the light, exclaims, "Wow, Zero, you ARE the most important!"

10 TENS 10¹	ONES 10⁰	1/10 TENTHS 10⁻¹	1/10×10 HUNDREDTHS 10⁻²	1/10×10×10 THOUS. 10⁻³

Deci interrupts, "Zero, you have

NO VALUE WITHOUT ME! When I move to the left

I make you worthless."

Finally Tenacious Ten interjects, "OK you two, knock it off! You are both important. We couldn't do without either one of you."

Doogie shakes his head, "Now I get why I should have paid attention in class.

This is why I didn't know the price of that basketball."

"Yes!" exclaims Ten as she and Doogie high-five.

"And you thought you'd never use this!"

Tenacious and her pals, Deci and Zero, to the rescue again!

Doogie returns to Nick's Sporting Goods store, pretending to be a new customer, this time wearing a fake mustache and glasses as a disguise.

With his new understanding of the value his money has, Doogie successfully pays the correct amount for his new leather basketball.

That's a SCORE for Doogie!

don't get it!"

As Tenacious Ten is leaving, there is a ringing sound from her pocket.

She pulls out her calculator-phone and a voice on the other end cries out, "The Metric System!

I JUST DON'T GET IT!"

Hearing her Call to Arms, Tenacious is gone in a flash of smoke...

Off to her next math rescue!

Teaching Tools:

This cautionary tale of "Doogie" represents a case of a typical student with math difficulty which classroom teachers frequently observe. While the concept of place value figures prominently in math instruction, all the way back to the primary grades, most students fail to realize the importance and the power of positional notation. A number's value is defined by its position relative to the decimal point. Memorization of math facts may proceed reasonably well without recognition of the big issues, but, understanding of quantity is not possible without understanding of this organization.

You can help bring this awareness of the workings of the system to light by examining the place value chart with your child. Have several (once is not enough to complete this job) conversations and ask your child to look for patterns in this format. For example: The number of factors of 10 moving from right to left. That number corresponds to the number of zeros following the one in each column's value.

Value: 10,000 1,000 100 10
Product: 10x10x10x10 10x10x10 10x10 10

Look at the exponential representation of the value of each column. Every exponent is the number of zeroes following the one. It is based on the number of times 10 is used as a factor.

Value: 10,000 1,000 100 10
Exponential Expressions: 14 103 102 101

There are many, many more of these which you and your child will discover with careful scrutiny. Extending your investigation to those same representations to the right of the decimal as well as exploring the metric system will bring more patterns to light. Make a game of it.

This portion of mathematics is really the Rosetta Stone of much of the instruction that will follow for your child. Helping them to a deep and thorough understanding of the language we use to represent math will give them a strong foundation on which to build their subsequent math skills.

Common Core Correlations*

In grade 2, instructional time should focus on four critical areas: (1) extending understanding of base-ten notation; (2) building fluency with addition and subtraction
(1)
Students extend their understanding of the base-ten system. This includes ideas of counting in fives, tens, and multiples of hundreds, tens and ones, as well as number relationships involving these units, including comparing. Students understand multi-digit numbers (up to 1000) written in base-ten notation, recognizing that the digits in each place represent amounts of thousands, hundreds, tens, or ones (e.g., 853 is 8 hundreds + 5 tens + 3 ones).
Understand place value.
1. Understand that the three digits of a three-digit number represent amounts of hundreds, tens, and ones; e.g., 706 equals 7 hundreds, 0 tens, and 6 ones. Understand the following as special cases: a. 100 can be thought of as a bundle of ten tens-- called a "hundred".
3. Read and write numbers to 1000 using base-ten numerals, number names, and expanded form.
4. Compare two three-digit numbers based on meanings of the hundreds, tens, and ones digits, using >, =, and < symbols to record the results comparisons.
Use place value understanding and properties of operations to add and subtract.
5. Fluently add and subtract within 100 using strategies based on place value, properties of operations, and/or the relationship between addition and subtraction.
In grade 4, instructional time should focus on:
(1)
Students generalize their understanding of place value to 1,000,000 understanding the relative sizes of numbers in each place. Students apply their understanding of models for division, place value, properties of operations, and the relationship of division to multiplication as they develop, discuss, and use efficient, accurate and generalizable procedures to find quotients involving multi-digit dividends. They select and accurately apply appropriate methods to estimate and mentally calculate quotients and interpret remainders based upon the context.
Generalize place value understanding for multi-digit whole numbers.
1. Recognize that in a multi-digit whole number, a digit in one place represents ten times what it represents in the place to its right. For example, recognize that $700 \div 70 = 10$ by applying concepts of place value and division.
2. Read and write multi-digit whole numbers using base-ten numerals, number names, and expanded form. Compare two multi-digit numbers based on meanings of the digits in each place, using >, =, and < symbols to record the results of comparisons.

*All references quoted from the Common Core Mathematics Standards

About the Authors:

Judy Newhoff has been a teacher for over 30 years and her passion has always been helping students appreciate and master the magic of numbers. Like Tenacious Ten, her greatest joy is found when she can work with a student to help that child better understand and appreciate how much fun math can be. In her spare time, Judy loves to be with family and is an avid hiker who has traversed the mountain trails of the Sierra-Nevada, the Andes, and the Himalayas.

Deanna Ruby Zevin comes from a family of writers and animators. She has been around children's story telling since she was a little girl and during her summers home from college she painted cartoons for television. Deanna's passion, however, was to be a teacher. She followed that passion and currently teaches math for 6th graders. Deanna was thrilled when she was able to convince her friend and colleague Judy Newhoff to co-write the tales of Tenacious Ten. When Deanna isn't teaching or writing, she loves to read, especially while sitting on the beach, by a lake, or in her pool.

About the Illustrator:

Kate Pitner is an illustrator and art teacher who loves picture books. If you take her to a book store you can be sure the children's section will be the first and last place you will find her. In addition to drawing pictures all day long, Kate loves peanut butter & chocolate ice cream, going to the beach, and imagining a world where math genius little girls appear out of nowhere and save the day! Kate lives in Los Angeles, California with her husband and two sons, along with her dog, Shamus, whom she believes leads a double life as a Super-Pooch.

Made in the USA
San Bernardino, CA
23 May 2019